JAVA
Interview
Questions

Aditya Chatterjee

Ue Kiao

1

Introduction

In this book "**Java Interview Questions**", we have presented several Interview Questions in Java (MCQ) covering all important topics in Java. These questions are frequently asked in Coding Interviews and you must attempt these questions. Each question is provided with the detailed answer.

This book is divided into four core sections:

- **Basic Java Interview Questions:** These are simple questions on background of Java.
- **Core Java Interview Questions**: These MCQs involve core Java ideas and are frequently asked in Coding Interviews.
- **Predict the Output Interview Questions**: In this section, you will be presented with a code snippet and you need to predict the output and answer related questions. These are common in Interviews and equally difficulty.

- **Descriptive Java Interview Questions**: These are advanced questions testing your understanding of Java ecosystem.

Each question is followed by a set of options. It is highly recommended that you answer the question on your own first by making notes on a sheet of paper and then, match your answer with the given answer. Go through the explanation for each answer.

Practice these questions to test your understanding of Java Programming Language. If you get an answer wrong, study the related topic in more depth.

Best of Luck for your Coding Interview.

Book: Java Interview Questions

Authors: Aditya Chatterjee, Ue Kiao

Published: February 2022

Publisher: OpenGenus

Contact & Feedback: team@opengenus.org

Table of contents

Other books you must read:

- Problems on Array: For Interviews and Competitive Programming
- Binary Tree Problems: Must for Interviews and Competitive Coding
- Time Complexity Analysis
- Dynamic Programming on Trees

- Day before Coding Interview series
- #7daysOfAlgo series

Basic Java Interview Questions

In this section, the questions revolve around the background of Java Programming Language and basic concepts.

When was Java released?

- 1996
- 2000
- 1995
- 2011

Answer: 1995

Java was first released in 23 May 1995 as a part of Sun Microsystem's Java platform.

What is the most common application of Java?

- Desktop applications
- Client Server web applications
- Web Servers
- Scripts

Answer: Client Server web applications

Client Server web applications is the most common application of Java. Over 9M programmers use Java actively for these applications. Java was marketed as a cross platform programming language and hence, was the driving force.

As of March 2022, what is the latest version of Java?

- Java 8
- Java SE
- Java 21
- Java 17

Answer: Java 17

Java 17 is the latest version which was released in October 2021. There are 3 long term supported versions of Java namely Java 8, Java 11 and Java 18.

Who owns Java?

- Sun Microsystems
- Oracle
- Google
- Microsoft

Answer: Oracle

As of 2022, Oracle owns Java. Java was originally developed and owned by Sun Microsystems who had the copyright on the name "Java" as well.

In 2009, Oracle acquired Sun Microsystems for $7.4B and Java came under Oracle.

Who was the core designer of Java?

- Mike Sheridan
- Patrick Naughton
- James Gosling
- Graydon Hoare

Answer: James Gosling

James Gosling is the core designer of Java who was the driving force behind the first release of Java in 1995. Mike Sheridan and

Patrick Naughton were involved in the Java project from the beginning which started in 1991.

James Gosling left Oracle in 2010.

What is the Java controversy between Oracle and Google?

Android which is a major project of Google internally leveraged the codebase of Java. Even though most of the code has been rewritten by Google developers to suit their use case, the API remains same as Java.

As Java was modified without the permission of Oracle who owns Java, Oracle registered a legal case against Google. The case continued for over a decade and is in active state. The major points are:

- If API can be copyrighted, then Google has done copyright infringement regarding Oracle's Java. It is in active discussion if API can be copyrighted but no conclusion has been formed.

- 2 rulings were in favor of Google and 1 was in favor of Oracle.

Name two environment variables that should be set to run Java programs.

The two environment variables are:

- PATH
- CLASSPATH

These should be set to compile and run the Java programs.

Is Java an OOP language?

- Yes
- No

Answer: No

Java is not a pure Object-Oriented Programming Language. This is because Java supports 8 primitive data types like Int, float, char and others which does not fit in the definition of OOP.

Hence, Java is not a pure OOP language.

What is wrapper class in Java?

Wrapper class in Java is a class that is used to convert a primitive datatype to an object. For example, if the primitive data type in "int", then the corresponding wrapper class in "Integer".

A wrapper class is used as follows;

```
public class Code {
    public static void main(String args[]) {
        int data = 1;
        Integer wrapperData =
Integer.valueOf(data);
    }
}
```

What is package in Java?

Package is a collection of classes, interfaces, libraries and JAR files which enables code reuse. It enables access protection and prevents naming conflicts.

Example of using a package in Java:

```
package examplePackage;
public class Code {
    public static void main(String args[]) {
        System.out.println("Java Interview");
    }
```

```
}
```

How to compile and run a Java program with a package?

If a Java program with filename "Code.java" and class name "Code" is within a package named "OG", then the compilation command will be:

```
javac -d directory Code.java
```

directory is the path of the package. It is this location where the compiled file will be placed.

To run the compiled class, use the following command:

```
java OG.Code
```

If there was no specific package, then the command to run the compiled class would be:

```
java Code
```

Can a constructor return a value?

In Java, a constructor cannot return a value explicitly.

Implicitly, a constructor in Java can update the current Class instance and, in this way, it can stimulate the behavior of returning a value.

What is super keyword in Java?

Super keyword is a reference keyword in Java that is used to refer to the immediate parent class. It can be used to invoke the parent class constructor with super() and refer to the parent class instance variable or method.

What is this keyword in Java?

this keyword is a reference keyword in Java like super keyword. this keyword is used to refer to the current class instance variable, method and constructor.

Example use of this keyword:

```
public int setData(int data) {
    this.data = data;
```

```
        return  this.data;
}
```

What is the life cycle of a thread in Java?

The five stages of the life cycle of a thread in Java are:

- New Born State
- Runnable State
- Running State
- Blocked State
- Dead State

What is the life cycle of a Java applet?

The five stages of the life cycle of an applet in Java are:

12

- Initialization
- Start
- Stop
- Destroy
- Paint

What are the types of access specifiers in Java?

The four types of access specifiers in Java are:

- Public Access Specifier
- Private Access Specifier
- Protected Access Specifier
- Default Access Specifier

Following image summarizes the differences:

Visibility	Default	Public	Protected	Private
Same class	Yes	Yes	Yes	Yes
Class in same package	Yes	Yes	Yes	No
Subclass in same package	Yes	Yes	Yes	No
Subclass outside the same package	No	Yes	Yes	No
Non-subclass outside the same package	No	Yes	No	No

What are the types of constructors in Java?

There are two types of constructors in Java:

- Parameterized Constructors: accept the parameters
- Default Constructors: does not accept the parameters

Core Java Interview Questions

In this section, the questions are based on core Java features and tests your ability to implement ideas in Java.

What is the size of boolean data type in Java?

- 1 bit
- 1 byte
- 2 bytes
- 4 bytes

Answer: 1 byte

Boolean data type is a primitive data type in Java and requires only 1 bit of memory. As 1 byte is the minimum assignable memory, the size of boolean data type is 1 byte (= 8 bits).

What is the default value of char data type in Java?

- ""
- u1111
- \u0000
- null

Answer: \u0000

The default value of char data type in Java is \u0000 which is known as the null character.

What is instance variable in Java?

- local to a method
- common to entire code
- with only one instance
- defined in main()

Answer: defined in main()

Instance variables are variables that have been defined in main() function. There are two other types of variables in Java which are "static variable" and "local variable".

What is the keyword used for Inheritance in Java?

- inherit
- extends
- implements
- clone

Answer: extends

"extends" is the keyword used for Inheritance in Java. "implements" keyword is used for using an Interface.

Following are the member variables in a standard HashMap implementation in Java:

```
static final int
DEFAULT_INITIAL_CAPACITY = 16;
static final int MAXIMUM_CAPACITY
= 1 << 30;
static final float
DEFAULT_LOAD_FACTOR = 0.75f;

transient Entry[] table;
transient int size;
int threshold;
final float loadFactor;
```

In the above code, what is meant by "transient"?

- Efficient transfer
- Local variable
- Enable Multi-threading
- Prevent Serialization

Answer: Prevent Serialization

transient keyword is used to avoid converting an object to a stream of bytes during serialization.

In Queue collection in Java, we can remove element using two standard member functions:

```
Queue<String> queue=new
PriorityQueue<String>();
// add
queue.add("opengenus");
// remove
queue.remove();
queue.poll();
```

What is the extra feature provided by queue.poll()?

- Return null if empty
- Does not return value
- Return type is boolean

- Thread safe removal

Answer: Return null if empty

queue.poll() is used to remove an element for Queue collection in Java. The difference from remove() is that poll() will return null if the Queue is empty while remove() will throw an error.

Which package is used to find the size of an object in Java?

Answer:
java.lang.instrument.Instrumentation

Instrumentation package in Java is used to instrument any Java code and get details of it. It is a common analysis technique which is natively supported in Java using the package. In short, in this technique, we insert code to the original code to track changes and performance. As changes are inserted, the original code remains unimpacted and hence, it is a good analysis tool.

To import this package, we need to use this:

```
import
java.lang.instrument.Instrumentation;
```

We have to create a Java class named ObjectSize to implement this. We can create a sizeof() function as follows:

```
public static long sizeof(Object o)
{
    return instrumentation.getObjectSize(o);
}
```

Which keyword is used to make resources thread-safe?

- wait
- sleep
- synchronized
- notify

Answer: synchronized

synchronized keyword is used to attain a lock on a resource, and make it thread-safe.

The threads go into which state if they do not get the desired resource?

- resumed
- active
- terminated
- waiting

Answer: waiting

The thread goes into waiting state, if it does not get its desired resource.

What is Static Initialization Block in Java?

A static block in a program is a set of statements which are executed by the JVM (Java Virtual Machine) before the main method. Java does not care if this block is written after the main() method or before the main() method, it will be executed before the main method() regardless.

```java
public  class Sample
{
    static{
        System.out.println("Hello World");
        System.exit(0);
    }
```

Note:

This code is working only on java versions up to 1.6. A newer version of Java does not support this feature anymore. We have to include the main method in our class with the static block.

What are the different types of control statements in Java?

Java has 3 different types of control statements:

- **Selection statements**: These statements give the option of choosing a different path of execution of a program depending on the result of a test condition. The expressions in this group are if, if-else and switch statement.

- **Iteration statements**: These statements allow repeated evaluation of a statement or a block of statements if the test condition is satisfied. This group contains a statement such as a while, do-while, for and for-each.
- **Jump statements**: These statements make the program control jump to another part of the program forward or backward directions with or without a test condition. The statements in this group are break, break label, continue.

What are the different types of References in Java?

There are 4 types of reference in Java Language:

- Strong Reference
- Weak Reference
- Soft Reference

- Phantom Reference

What is Soft Reference in Java?

Soft References are a special kind of reference, which slightly changes the default behavior of the Garbage Collector, allowing the GC to maintain objects without strong references until the Java Virtual Machine runs out of memory. In this last case, the Garbage Collector will try to save the application scanning the memory and deleting all the soft references.

Code snippet of Soft Reference in Java:

```java
import java.lang.ref.*

// ...

Object obj = new Object();

// New Soft Reference to obj object
```

```
SofReference<Object> softRef = new
SoftReference<Object>(obj);
```

Strings are immutable in Java. What are the advantages?

The advantages of having Strings as immutable in Java includes:

- Caching
- Hashcode Caching
- Better Performance
- Synchronization
- Security

What is Anonymous class?

Java Anonymous inner class is an inner class without a name and for which only a single object is created. It works just like the local class; all restrictions remain the same for its members.

You can declare the following inside an anonymous class.

- Property (fields)
- Methods (Only instance methods), even if they do not implement any methods of the supertype.
- Instance initializer
- Local classes

What is Double brace initialization?

Double brace initialization is a combination of two separate process in java. There are two { braces involved in it. If you see two consecutive curly braces { in java code, it is an usage of double brace initialization. First brace is creation of an anonymous inner class. Second brace is an initialization block. When you use the initialization block for an anonymous inner class it becomes java double brace initialization.

Let us see its implementation:

```java
/*Here we will create a list in which the
elements are
stored with the help of double brace
initialization.*/
import java.util.*;
public class Main{
    public static void main(String[] args){
        List <Integer> list = new
ArrayList<>()
        {{
            // Double Brace Initialization
            add(56);
            add(67);
            add(90);
            add(78);
            add(35);
        }};
        // print the list
        System.out.println(list);
    }
}
```

Output:

`[56, 67, 90, 78, 35]`

What is encapsulation?

The wrapping up of data and functions (that operate on the data) into a single unit (called class) is known as encapsulation

The only way to access the data is provided by the function (that are combined along with the data). These functions are called member functions or methods in Java. The data cannot be accessed directly. If you want to read a data item in an object (an instance of class), you call a member function in the object. It will read the item and return the value to you. You cannot access the data directly. The data is hidden, so it is safe from accidental alteration. Data and its functions are said to be encapsulated into a single entity.

How to create a directory in Java?

To create a directory:

- Create the object of the File class by passing the path of the directory, as a parameter (String) to the constructor of the File class
- call the mkdir() method using the above created file object

Example of Java code to create a directory using mkdir() method.

```java
import java.io.File;
public class CreateDirectory{
    public static void main(String args[]){
        //creating a File object
        File file = new
File(F:\\program);
        //creating the directory
        boolean bool = file.mkdir();
        if(bool){
            System.out.println("Directory
created successfully");
```

```
        }else{
            System.out.println("Directory not
created");
        }
    }
}
```

How to delete non empty Folders Recursively in Java?

In Java, we cannot delete folder that are not empty. The workaround is to delete all files first using delete() utility and then, recursively delete empty folders using delete() utility starting from the inner most folders.

delete() function can be used recursively to delete non-empty folders/ directory. We can define a recursive function named recursiveDelete() which will:

- check if the current location is a file or folder
- If it is a file, then it will be deleted
- If it is an empty folder, it will be deleted
- If it is not an empty folder, it will go through all objects within the folder and apply the function recursively

Follow this function carefully:

```java
import java.io.File;
public class DeleteFolderRecursively {
    public static void main(String[] args) {
        String folder = "F:\\program";
        //delete folder recursively
        recursiveDelete(new File(folder));
    }

    public static void recursiveDelete(File file) {
        //to end the recursive loop
        if (!file.exists())
            return;

        //if directory, go inside and call recursively
        if (file.isDirectory()) {
            for (File f : file.listFiles()) {
                //call recursively
                recursiveDelete(f);
```

```
                }
            }
            //call delete to delete files and empty
directory
            file.delete();
            System.out.println("Deleted
file/folder: "+file.getAbsolutePath());
        }


}
```

Among String, StringBuffer and StringBuilder, which is the fastest?

- String
- StringBuilder
- StringBuffer
- Same time for all

Answer: StringBuilder

StringBuilder is not thread safe or
synchronized and does not create a new

object when modified, hence it is the fastest among the three options. The second fastest is StringBuffer which is threadsafe while String is the slowest as a new object is created every time it is modified.

Following is a sample Java implementation of Singleton class:

```java
// Singleton class in Java
public final class ClassSingleton {
    private static ClassSingleton INSTANCE;
    private String info = "Initial info class";

    private ClassSingleton() {
    }

    public static ClassSingleton getInstance() {
        if(INSTANCE == null) {
            INSTANCE = new ClassSingleton();
        }
        return INSTANCE;
```

```
        }
    }
}
```

What is the issue with the above Java code for Singleton class?

- Static instance not created
- constructor should be public
- Not thread safe
- Serializable not supported

Answer: Not thread safe

It is not thread safe so synchronized keyword must be used with method definition getInstance().

How we can explicitly call Garbage Collector in Java?

- System.gc()
- System.exit(2)

- Not possible
- Allocate large amount of memory

Answer: System.gc()

System.gc() can be used to explicitly call Garbage Collector in Java. Note that this call only suggests the Garbage Collector to run so there may be a case where Garbage Collector will not run if it does not find it necessary.

There are 3 phases in Garbage Collector in Java. Which one of these is not one of the 3 phases?

- Major
- Minor
- Mark-copy
- Full

Answer: Mark-copy

Mark-copy is a Garbage Collection algorithm which is used in specific cases. There are three main phases in Garbage Collector in Java: Major, Minor and Full.

There are 4 types of References in Java. Weak Reference in Java is defined as follows:

```
// Creates a strong reference
Object obj = new Object();
// New Weak Reference to obj
object
WeakReference<Object> softRef =
new WeakReference<Object>(obj);
```

When is an object having a weak reference removed by the Garbage Collector?

- Only if memory is needed

 OPENGENUS

- Never
- Always
- Varies across runtime

Answer: Always

Weak References have another interpretation from the Garbage Collector. While the types mentioned before are, for default, preserved in memory, if an object has only a weak reference attached to him when the GC is running, then it will be reclaimed even if the virtual machine doesn't need more space.

If an object has a strong reference, then it is never removed by the Garbage Collector. A strong reference is defined as follows:

```
Object obj = new Object();
// Creates a strong reference
```

How is a strong reference to an object removed?

- obj.remove()
- System.gc()
- System.exit(obj)
- obj = null

Answer: obj = null

Using "obj = null", the strong reference to the object obj is removed and the object obj is available for Garbage Collector to remove it to make memory available.

In Java Collections, there are several variants of HashMap of which following are two variants:

```
Map<String, Integer> map =
        new HashMap<String,
Integer>();
```

```
LinkedHashMap<Integer, String>
lhmap =
      new LinkedHashMap<Integer,
String>();
```

What is the additional property of LinkedHashMap over HashMap?

- Maintains order of elements
- Synchronized
- Thread safe
- Serializable

Answer: Maintains order of elements

LinkedHashHap is an implementation of HashMap which uses Linked List for chaining. It maintains the order of elements based on insertion order and can be traversed as such. HashMap does not maintain the order.

What is the default load factor of HashMap collection in Java?

- 0.25f
- 0.50f
- 0.75f
- 0.95f

Answer: 0.75f

Load factor is the fraction of memory already utilized in HashMap so that at this point, the HashMap is resized and the memory is doubled. The load factor by default is 0.75f in HashMap collection in Java. It is captured by the member variable DEFAULT_LOAD_FACTOR in the implementation of HashMap.

Which type of Inheritance is not possible in Java?

- Multi-level

- Multiple Inheritance
- All are possible

Answer: Multiple Inheritance

Multiple Inheritance is not permitted in Java but it can be implemented using Interface.

throw and throws are different keywords in Java and are used in different places to raise an exception.

Which one is used to raise an exception always?

- throw
- throws
- None
- Depends on implementation

Answer: throw

throw is used to raise an exception always and is used within a function while "throws" is used in method signature and is used as a signal that the function may raise an error.

In Java, the Collections library is present in which package?

- java.util
- java.lang
- java.io
- java.system

Answer: java.util

java.util is the package for the various Collections in Java like HashMap.

There are two ways to support Multi-threading in Java: Thread and

Runnable. Which one is used by inheritance?

- Runnable
- Thread
- None
- Both

Answer: Thread

To support Multi-threading, we need to inherit Thread class or implement the Runnable interface. It is recommended to use Runnable as on using Thread class, we cannot inherit any other class as Multiple Inheritance is not supported in Java.

What is the compiler name of Java?

- gcc
- aocc
- javac
- java virtual machine

Answer: javac

javac is the compiler for Java. A code file named code.java is compiled using the command "javac code.java".

Following code shows the use of static keyword in two different ways:

```java
public class PrintWord {

  // Static variable
  static float check_variable1 =
1.02;

  void function_check() {
    // Local variable
    double check_variable2 =
2.931271;
  }

  public static void main(final
String[] args) {
    // Instance variable
```

```
    int check_variable3 = 2;
  }
}
```

What is static keyword used in Java for?

- Immutable reference
- Mutable reference
- One common copy

Answer: One common copy

static keyword is used when we want to keep one common copy across all instances of a class and different functions. Note main() is used with static as there is only one main().

Which of the following cleans the permanent memory space?

- Major GC
- Minor GC
- Full GC
- None of these

Answer: None of these

Minor GC cleans the Eden memory space while Major GC cleans the Old generation memory space. Full GC cleans both Eden and Old Generation Memory space. Hence, none of the three GC phases clean the permanent memory space.

Which of the following is the slowest process?

- Full GC
- Major GC
- Minor GC
- All takes equal time

Answer: Full GC

Full Garbage collection involves both Major and Minor GC so it takes the longest amount of time.

Where is a newly declared variable allocated memory?

- Survivor 1 space
- Survivor 0 space
- Eden space
- Old generation space

Answer: Eden Space

All new variables are allocated memory from Eden space. If there is no space left in Eden space, then a Minor Garbage Collection is used to make space available.

Why is Java not purely Object Oriented Programming (OOP) language?

- Strings are immutable objects
- Java is OOP
- Due to lambda in Java

Answer: Primitive datatypes are not objects

Java is not a pure Object-Oriented Programming (OOP) language because Primitive datatypes are not objects whereas in OOP, everything should be an object.

Pointers is a concept in C and C++ which is not available in Java. Pointer is used to access memory directly. It is not supported in Java to make the language memory safe.

Who manages memory in Java?

- JVM
- JDK
- User code
- JRE

Answer: JVM

JVM has the responsibility to manage memory and allocate as and when required.

Java is known for its code portability / write once run anywhere. JIT compiler known as Just In Time Compiler plays a major role.

What is the role of JIT compiler?

- Code to Bytecode
- Bytecode to Machine Code
- Runtime optimizations
- Remove non-portable code

Answer: Bytecode to Machine Code

JIT compiler is used to convert the bytecode to machine code. The bytecode is machine-independent while the machine code varies across systems. It is the bytecode which makes Java platform independent.

What keyword is used to prevent a class from being extended / inherited?

- const
- final
- =0
- void static

Answer: final

final keyword is used to define a class which cannot be extended or inherited by any other class in Java. final keyword has similar use case in defined variables and methods.

In Inheritance in Java, super() is used to access methods of the parent or base class.

Which keyword is used to access methods of the current class?

- -->
- static
- this()
- Use with super()

Answer: this()

this() is used to access methods of the current class which super() is used to access methods of the parent or base class.

Why is there a String Pool in Java but not Integer Pool for int?

- int is primitive datatype
- Design principle
- String is array of char
- String is immutable

Answer: String is immutable

Memory Pool is created for all immutable objects. As string is immutable, String Pool exists. On the other hand, as int is a mutable data type, there is not memory pool for int.

What is the process of calling one constructor from another constructor called?

- Constructor Inheritance
- Constructor fallback
- Constructor chaining
- Polymorphism

Answer: Constructor chaining

Constructor chaining is the process of calling one constructor from another constructor. This involves the use of this() and super() keywords.

String is immutable and stored in its special area called String Pool. The alternative to string is StringBuffer and StringBuilder.

Where are StringBuffer and StringBuilder stored?

- String Pool
- Heap area
- Eden space
- Old generation space

Answer: Heap area

StringBuffer and StringBuilder are mutable objects so they are stored in Heap area.

What is Polymorphism in Java?

- Hide details
- One interface, many implementations
- Use common interface
- Use abstract class

Answer: One interface, many implementations

Polymorphism refers to the OOP concept of One interface, many implementations. There are two types of Polymorphism: Runtime and Compile-time.

Multiple Inheritance is not supported in Java. Why?

- Source of several bugs

- To be added in future
- Major limitation of Java
- Memory layout does not support

Answer: Source of several bugs

Multiple Inheritance is not supported in Java because Multiple Inheritance is not considered a good practice and results in complex code and several bugs in practice. For this, this is restricted in Java. A similar design can be implemented using Interfaces. This problem is known as Diamond Problem.

What is Copy Constructor?

- Constructor with parameters
- Constructor in inherited class
- Constructor with no parameters
- Initialize object using another object

Answer: Initialize object using another object

Copy Constructor is a constructor that is used to initialize the new object by copying parameters of another object.

finally block is a block of code statements that always execute and is associated with a try catch statement. When will a finally block not execute?

- System.gc()
- System.exit()
- Multi-threads
- Memory corruption

Answer: System.exit()

finally block not execute in case of System.exit() or a fatal error.

OutOfMemoryError is an object and not just an error statement. It is an object of which class?

- java.lang.Error
- java.util.Error
- java.lang
- java.io.Error

Answer: java.lang.Error

OutOfMemoryError is an object of java.lang.Error class. In OOP, everything should be an object ideally.Only exception in Java are primitive data types.

If a program goes in an unexpected direction, then Error or Exception can occur. Which one can a Programmer handle in code?

- Error
- Exception
- None
- Both

Answer: Exception

Exception can be handled using try and catch block but an Error cannot be handled in code. Exception occurs due to unexpected input or behavior and this can be detected and an alternative path can be taken or execution can be terminated.

Among String, StringBuilder and StringBuffer, which one is not thread safe?

- StringBuilder
- String
- StringBuffer
- None

Answer: StringBuilder

StringBuilder is not thread safe but is more efficient than String as StringBuilder is mutable and new objects are not created during its modification.

Why are packages used in Java?

- Code organization
- Access Specifier
- For creating library
- Prevent name conflicts

Answer: Prevent name conflicts

Package in Java is used to prevent name conflicts across methods.

Predict Output of Code

In this section, each question will have a Java code snippet along with four options. You need to predict the output of the code snippet.

First try to predict the output irrespective of the options provided. Remember there will be cases where the code may give a compilation or runtime error and you need to predict this along with the reasoning.

Each question is followed by the correct answer along with the detailed explanation.

What is the output of the following code snippet?

```java
String og = "opengenus";
String og2 = new String(og);

System.out.println((og==og2) + "
"+ (og.equals(og2)));
```

- true true
- true false
- false true
- false false

Answer: false true

The operator == compare the address of the two variables while equals method compare the content of the two variables.

What is the output of the following code snippet?

```
int five = 5;
int two = 2;
int total = five + (five > 6 ?
++two : --two);
```

- 1
- 2

- 4
- 6

Answer: 6

In ternary expressions, only one of the two right-most expressions are evaluated. Since "five" > 6 is false, —"two" is evaluated and ++"two" is skipped. "two" is changed from 2 to 1 and total becomes "five" + (1) which means 5 + 1 = 6.

Which one is not a valid statement in Java?

```
double num = 2.718;
double num = 2._718;
double num = 2.7_1_8;
```

Answer: double num = 2._718;

Underscore (_) is valid between two numbers but in this code statement, underscore is between a number and dot (.). Hence, it is the only code statement that is not valid and will not compile.

How many strings can be collected by Garbage Collector in the following code snippet?

```
public static void main(String[]
fruits) {
   String str1 = new
String("open");
   String str2 = new
String("source");
   String str2 = new
String("opengenus");
   str3 = str1;
   str2 = str3;
   str1 = str2;
}
```

- 0
- 1
- 2
- 3

Answer: 2

All three strings (str1, str2, str3) point to the same string that is "open". Hence, the two strings str2 and str3 can be collected by Garbage Collector before the end of main() function.

What is the output of the following code snippet?

```
Integer int_data = new Integer(10);
System.out.print(int_data.byteValue());
System.out.print("-");
int int_data_2 = new Integer(10);
System.out.print(int_data_2.byteValue());
```

66

- 10-10
- 1010-1010
- Does not compile
- Run-time error

Answer: Compilation error

If you compile the above code snippet, you will get the following compilation error:

```
opengenus.java:11: error: int cannot
be dereferenced
System.out.print (int_data_2.byteValue ( ) )
;
                                         ^
Note: opengenus.java uses or
overrides a deprecated API.
Note: Recompile with -
Xlint:deprecation for details.
```

```
1 error
```

byteValue() is for Integer wrapper dataype and not for the int primitive datatype.

What is the output of the following code snippet?

```
double d1 = 5f; // c1
double d2 = 5.0; // c2
float f1 = 5f; // c3
float f2 = 5.0; // c4
```

- c1
- c2
- c3
- c4

Answer: c4

The problem with the last code statement is that it attempts to convert a double (5.0) to a float which will result in accuracy loss. Hence, this will result in compilation error.

What is the output of the following code snippet?

```java
public static void main(String... args) {
    String car, bus = "petrol";
    car = car + bus;
    System.out.println(car);
}
```

- petrol
- petrolpetrol
- Compilation error
- Runtime error

Answer: Compilation error

 © OPENGENUS

If you compile the above code snippet, you will get the following compilation error:

```
opengenus.java:4: error:
 variable car might not have
been initialized
    car = car + bus;
        ^
1 error
```

In the code snippet, the car variable remains uninitialized while "petrol" is assigned to bus variable only.

What is the output of the following code snippet?

```
double num1, int num2 = 1; // C1
int num1, num2; // C2
int num1, num2 = 1; // C3
int num1 = 2, num2 = 1; // C4
```

- C1
- C2
- C3
- C4

Answer: C1

Java does not permit programmers to declare different data types in the same declaration. Hence, the first code statement C1 does not compile correctly.

What is the output of the following code snippet?

```
public  class Test {
          public static void main(String[]
args) {
                   for(int  i=0;  0;  i++) {
```

```
            System.out.println("Hello
World!");
                        }
            }
}
```

- Hello World!
- no output
- Compilation error
- Runtime error

Answer: Compilation error

```
opengenus.java:3: error:
incompatible types:
int cannot be converted to boolean
                for(int i=0; 0; i++) {
                              ^

1 error
```

0 does not convert to boolean value.

What is the output of the following code snippet?

```
public class Code {
        public static void main(String[]
args) {
                for(int i = 0; i < 1;
i++) {

        System.out.println(i+' ');
                }
        }
}
```

- 1
- 0
- 32
- 50

Answer: 32

The answer is a character code as 0 is appended with a character ' ' and the result should be a character so, the character '1' is converted the numeric character code that is 32.

What is the output of the following code snippet?

```java
public  class Code {
        public static void main(String[] args)
    {
            if (true)
                break;
    }
}
```

- No output
- 0
- Compilation error

- Runtime error

Answer: Compilation error

On compiling the code, you will get the following error:

```
opengenus.java:5: error: break
outside switch
   or loop
                break;
                ^
1 error
```

In Java, break statement can be used within loop like for, while or do while loop or within switch statement. Hence, the code snippet produces compilation error.

What is the output of the following code snippet?

```java
public  class Code {
    public static void main(String[] args)
    {
        int $_ = 5;
    }
}
```

- No output
- 0
- Compilation error
- Runtime error

Answer: No output

In Java, an identifier can start with an alphabet, underscore (_) or dollar sign ($). Hence, $_ is a valid identifier/ variable in this case.

What is the output of the following code snippet?

```java
public  class Code{
    public static void main(String[] arr){

    }
    public static void main(String arr){

    }
}
```

- No output
- 0
- Compilation error
- Runtime error

Answer: No output

main() function can be overloaded in Java. The main() function that has String[] will be the entry point and will be called by Java.

What is the output of the following code snippet?

```java
public  class Code {
    public static void main(String[] args)
    {
            System.out.println('j' + 'a' +
'v' + 'a');
        }
}
```

- java
- 32
- 418
- Compilation error

Answer: 418

As each character is enclosed in single quotes, it is considered as a character and not a string by Java. Hence, the concatenation will result in a character. As the string "java" cannot fit in a character, the characters are converted to ASCII value before concatenation that is addition.

106 + 97 + 118 + 97 = 418

What is the output of the following code snippet?

```
public class Code{
    public static void main(String[] arr){
        Integer num1 = 400;
        Integer num2 = 400;

        if(num1 == num2){
            System.out.println(0);
        }
        else{
            System.out.println(1);
        }
```

```
        }
    }
}
```

- 0
- 1
- Compilation error
- Runtime error

Answer: 1

Integer class support the range of -128 to 127. If the number is within the range, autoboxing is applied. This means the same reference is assigned for the same number as they are from the same pool. As 400 is outside the range, different references are assigned.

What is the output of the following code snippet?

```java
public  class Code {
    public static void main(String[] args)
{
        method(null);
    }
    public static void method(Object o) {
        System.out.println("Object
method");
    }
    public static void method(String s) {
        System.out.println("String
method");
    }
}
```

- Object method
- String method
- Compilation error
- Runtime error

Answer: String method

Null is not an object in Java.

Java compiler prefer the method which has more specific parameters.

String is object of the class java.lang.String. Hence, String is more specific than Object class. Therefore, null is matched as a string object.

What is the output of the following code snippet?

```
class Code {
    String args[] = { "1", "2" };
    public static void main(String args[])
    {

System.out.println(args.length);
    }
}
```

- 0
- 1
- 2
- 3

Answer: 0

args is the command line arguments and is not related to the global variable args. So, if you run the above code without passing any command line argument, you will get the output as 0.

What is the output of the following code snippet?

```
class Code {
    public static void main(String args[])
    {
        System.out.println(value());
    }
    int value() {
        return 1;
    }
}
```

- 0
- 1

- Compilation error
- Runtime error

Answer: Compilation error

Following is the compilation error on compiling the above code:

```
opegenus.java:3: error: non-
static method value()
 cannot be referenced from a static context
    System.out.println(value());
                              ^

1 error
```

The problem is that in Java, we cannot call a non-static function from a static function. Therefore, the fix is to make the function value() static.

The correct Java code is:

```java
class Code {
    public static void main(String args[])
{
        System.out.println(value());
    }
    static int value() {
        return 1;
    }
}
```

What is the output of the following code snippet?

```java
class Code {
    public static void main(String args[]) {
        System.out.println(value());
    }
    static int value() {
        static int data = 0;
        return data;
    }
}
```

- 0
- 1
- Compilation error
- Runtime error

Answer: Compilation error

Following is the compilation error on compiling the above code:

```
opengenus.java:6: error:
illegal start of expression
        static int data = 0;
        ^

opengenus.java:7: error:
illegal start of type
        return data;
        ^

opengenus.java:7: error:
<identifier> expected
        return data;
```

```
opengenus.java:9: error: class,
interface, or enum expected
}
^
4 errors
```

The problem is that in Java, we cannot have static local variables. The alternative is to use static class members.

The fix will be to change "data" variable to be non-static or make "data" variable a static class member.

What is the output of the following code snippet?

```java
class Parent {
    public void Print()
    {
        System.out.println("Parent");
    }
}
```

```
}

class Child extends Parent {
    public void Print()
    {
            System.out.println("Child");
    }
}

class Main {
    public static void PrintMain(Parent
o)
    {
            o.Print();
    }
    public static void main(String[] args)
    {
            Parent x = new Parent();
            Parent y = new Child();
            Child z = new Child();
            PrintMain(x);
            PrintMain(y);
            PrintMain(z);
    }
}
```

- Child, Child, Child

- Parent, Child, Child
- Parent, Child, Parent
- Parent, Parent, Child

Answer: Parent, Child, Child

The first print statement prints "Parent" as the parent reference is passed to it.

The second print statement prints "Child" because of run time polymorphism which is enabled in Java by default.

The third print statement is passed the reference of Child and hence, the print statement of Child is called. Note that the concept of object slicing which is present in C++ is not valid in Java.

What is the output of the following code snippet?

```java
public  class Code {
    public static void main(String[] args)
{
        method(null);
    }
    public static void method(Object o) {
        System.out.println("Object method");
    }
    public static void method(Integer i) {
        System.out.println("Integer method");
    }
    public static void method(String s) {
        System.out.println("String method");
    }
}
```

- Object method
- String method
- Integer method
- Compilation error

Answer: Compilation error

The code gives the following compilation error:

```
opengenus.java:3: error:
reference to method is
ambiguous
        method(null);
        ^
  both method method(Integer)
in Code and method
method(String) in Code match
1 error
```

Null is not an object in Java.

Java compiler prefer the method which has more specific parameters.

String is object of the class java.lang.String. Hence, String is more specific than Object class but it is equally specific to Integer class. Therefore, null is unable to match to any function as it is unable to choose between String and Integer.

What is the output of the following code snippet?

```java
public class Code
{
    public static void main(String args[])
    {
        StringBuffer str1 = new StringBuffer("open");
        StringBuffer str2 = str1;
        str1.append("genus");
        System.out.println(str1 + " "
+ str2 + " " + (str1 == str2));
    }
}
```

- opengenus open false
- opengenus opengenus false

- opengenus open true
- opengenus opengenus true

Output: opengenus opengenus true

This is because StringBuffer objects are mutable. str2 is pointing to str1 object and not a copy of str1. So, when str1 is modified, str2 points to it so its value is also modified.

If we replace StringBuffer with String, output will be "opengenus open false" as String objects are not mutable and new objects are created when we modified them.

What is the output of the following code snippet?

```
public  class Code
{
    public static void main(String args[])
    {
        int  y  =  08;
```

```
        y = y + 2;
        System.out.println(y);
    }
}
```

- 8
- 9
- Compilation error
- Runtime error

Answer: Compilation error

The code will give the following compilation error:

```
opengenus.java:5: error: integer
 number too large
        int y = 08;
              ^
1 error
```

Any number starting with 0 is considered an octal number which has digits from 0 to 7. So, 08 is invalid and hence, the code will fail to compile.

What is the output of the following code snippet?

```
class Code extends Thread
{
    public void run()
    {
        System.out.print("thread 1");
    }
    public static void main(String args[])
    {
        Code thread1 = new Code();
        thread1.start();
        thread1.stop();
        thread1.start();
    }
}
```

- 8
- 9
- Compilation error
- Runtime error

Answer: Runtime error

The code will give the following runtime error:

```
Exception in thread "main"
java.lang.IllegalThreadStateException at
java.lang.Thread.start
```

The issue is that a thread cannot be started twice.

What is the output of the following code snippet?

```
class CodeA
```

```
{
    public String type = "A ";
    public CodeA() {
        System.out.print("CodeA ");
    }
}

public  class CodeB extends CodeA
{
    public CodeB() {
        System.out.print("CodeB ");
    }

    void go()
    {
        type = "B ";
        System.out.print(this.type +
super.type);
    }

    public static void main(String[] args)
    {
        new  CodeB().go();
    }
}
```

- CodeA CodeB A B

- CodeA CodeA B B
- CodeA CodeB B B
- CodeB CodeB B B

Answer: CodeA CodeB B B

CodeB().go() executes in two phases:

- CodeB class constructor is called followed by CodeA class constructor as CodeB extends CodeA.
- go() function is called on CodeB object which overrides the variable "type" to B and hence, the same value "B" is printed twice. In this code snippet, super keyword is not playing any role.

What is the output of the following code snippet?

```
public  class Code
{
    public static void main(String[] args)
    {
```

```
        Integer a = 128, b = 128;
        System.out.println(a == b);

        Integer c = 100, d = 100;
        System.out.println(c == d);
    }
}
```

- true true
- false false
- false true
- true false

Answer: false true

In the function valueOf() in Integer, the range is -128 (IntegerCache.low) to 127 (IntegerCache.high) so numbers outside this range will not give expected result. Therefore, the objects will value 100 equates to be equal.

Descriptive Java Interview Questions: Advanced

This section covers the most advanced Java questions that are asked in Coding Interviews which several beginner programmers find difficult to answer correctly.

Name some Industry Standard Performance Benchmark for Java.

Some Industry Standard Performance Benchmark for Java are:

- SPECcpu
- SPECvirt_sc
- SPECjbb
- SPECjvm
- SPECjEnterprise

Name some Application Profilers for Java.

Some Application Profilers for Java are:

- VisualVM
- JRockit Mission Control
- Oracle Solaris Studio Performance Analyzer

What flags are used to enable JRE profiling and debug information?

Flags are used to enable JRE profiling and debug information are:

- -XX:+PrintCompilation
- -verbose:gc
- -verbose:class
- -Xprintflags

Name some Hardware Counters for Java applications.

Some Hardware Counters for Java applications are:

- Sun Studio Performance Analyzer
- oprofile
- VTune

Name some tools to profile the entire system while running a Java application.

Some tools and commands to profile the entire system while running a Java application are:

- top
- htop
- vmstat
- mpstat
- iostat

- dtrace
- strace

These are general commands and can be used to profile entire system while running any application beyond Java.

What is JavaOne?

JavaOne was an annual conference by Sun Microsystems to discuss Java technologies. It was first organized in 1996 and was one of the most popular conferences of its time.

Every conference featured a hardware device where Java is used. In 1998, it featured a finger ring which had Java embedded microprocessor.

In 1999, it has more than 20,000 attendees. Later as Sun Microsystems was acquired by Oracle, JavaOne was discontinued in 2018 and replaced by Oracle Code One which involves other technologies as well.

Name some Programming Languages other than Java that used JVM.

Some Programming Languages other than Java that used JVM are:

- BeanShell
- Clojure
- Groovy
- JRuby
- Jython
- Kotlin
- Processing
- Rhino
- Scala
- Oxygene

Name two Conferences focused on Java exclusively.

Two major Conferences that are focused exclusively to Java are:

- JavaOne
- Devoxx

What is JCA in Java?

JCA stands for Java Cryptography Architecture.

Java Cryptography Architecture is the platform, architecture and API for encryption and decryption in Java applications. JCA is used as a security measure and is used to enforced security rules. It has support for hash table, encryption message digest and much more.

What is JPA in Java?

JPA stands for Java Persistence API.

Java Persistence API is used to add support of persistence layer for Java applications. JPA includes:

- Java Persistence API
- Query Language
- Java Persistence Criteria API
- Object Mapping Metadata

How to generate Stack Trace in Java?

The following two statements can be used to generate stack trace of a Java program:

- Throwable().printStackTrace() for stack trace of a method at a point.
- Thread.currentThread.dumpStack() for stack trace of a current thread.

Example Java code snippet using Throwable().printStackTrace():

```java
public static boolean download( String url)
{
    ........
    // If the download succeeded.
    if (success)
    {
        // see if the correct number of bytes
        were copied
        long newFileLength = new
        File(targetFile).length();
        if (expectedSize !=
        newFileLength)
        {
            Debug.trace(1, url);
            Throwable().printStackTrace();
            return false;
        }
    }
    else
    {
        Debug.trace(1, url);
        return false;
    }
    ........
    return true;
}
```

What is Jikes in Java?

Jikes is an alternative to javac and is an open-source Java compiler developed by IBM. It is a high performing compiler but the user interface is limited and hence, is not widely used in general. It is used by IBM internally and for specific Java applications.

In Jikes:

- Compiler is invoked by jikes command
- Debugger is invoked by jd command

What is Java Swing?

Java Swing is a component of Java Foundation Classes which is used for Graphical User Interfaces.

Swing is used to create window based applications like desktop applications. It is built on top of an abstract windowing toolkit (AWT) API and is purely written in Java.

Java Swing is an alternative to Java AWT.

What are Java Applets?

Java applets are Java programs that can be embedded in a HTML page and run on the browser when pages are visited. It provides interactive features to web applications and can be executed by browsers on any platform.

This was one of the core features of Java to make it cross platform and was a driving feature for its initial success.

What is Java Beans?

Java Beans is a class that encapsulates many objects into one object so that it can be accessed from a single object. It is a Java technology that was first released in 1996 with JDK1.1.

With this, you must have a good practice in questions in Java Programming Language. Best of luck for your Examination or Coding Interview.

For more practice and to contribute to Computing Community, feel free to join our Internship Program:

internship.OPENGENUS.org